Lilacs

Lilacs

Poems by

Mary-Michelle DeCoste

© 2021 Mary-Michelle DeCoste. All rights reserved.
This material may not be reproduced in any form, published,
reprinted, recorded, performed, broadcast,
rewritten or redistributed without
the explicit permission of Mary-Michelle DeCoste.
All such actions are strictly prohibited by law.

Cover design by Shay Culligan
Cover image by Annie Spratt
Author image by Trina Koster

ISBN: 978-1-63980-056-8

Kelsay Books
502 South 1040 East, A-119
American Fork, Utah 84003
Kelsaybooks.com

Acknowledgments

The Road Not Taken: "Lilacs"

Shot Glass Journal: "About My Son," "(The cleaner)," "Homecoming"

Mezzo Cammin: "Is That All There Is?," "Mistaken Identity"

The Lyric: "The Bathroom Door," "The Stingy Carver"

Third Wednesday: "Roommates"

Contents

Lilacs	11
Marigolds	12
Forsythia	13
About My Son	14
Sore Feet	15
Mother, Making Ends Meet	16
Captain	17
Emergency Preparedness	18
Main Street	19
Italian Movie Star	21
Is That All There Is?	22
Mistaken Identity	23
The Bathroom Door	24
The Stingy Carver	25
Facing-Page Translation	26
Homecoming	27
Guest	28
In Costa Rica	29
The cleaner, brusque, pressed	30
Sometimes, Going in Circles Is the Way Out	31
A Vision	32
Animal	33
Roommates	34
Marrow	36
Freedom	37

Lilacs

As heavy as a pregnancy, as love,
sweet as a child before she's learned to speak,
they hung themselves, the gobs of purple blooms
among the green and glossy heart-shaped leaves,
until he said—The lilacs should be pruned.
All living things grow better when they're cut
from time to time, and now is not too soon.—
My mother bit her tongue, but I could not.
Grandfather laughed at me—They will grow back,
whether or not you want them to, in June.—
In June, just a probationary shoot
that swayed a gentle caution, gentle yearning.
I'm grateful that the lilacs sent a warning.
I'm hopeful something's waiting at the root.

Marigolds

You wanted marigolds, Grandfather, so you jammed them in
everywhere there was dirt.

Only after you had died did she say
she never liked marigolds much.
She liked petunias but
did not want to interfere with your pleasure
so she put up with the marigolds.

Daughters do things like this, sometimes.

When you cracked the door and caught me
still sleeping next to my boyfriend, you
told her I was running around.

Grandfather, you ought to have understood my running,
you who left your mother behind
in Ireland's damp and grey,
who when your wife held your son in her arms,
and the doctor said another pregnancy would kill her,
did not stop
and it nearly did
and that was my mother.

So now when my lover whispers to me,
Marigold, Marigold,
I sometimes think of you
without affection.

Forsythia

The forsythia pushed from the spring earth
ordinary as milk and kisses
spilling abundance over itself
so that the children
could part the branches
and enter into another world

in which
the mothers and fathers were very far away
almost as if
they no longer existed at all.
The children looked at each other
and drew their knees to their chests.

When they cut it down,
the mothers and fathers did not know
that they had come back from the dead.

About My Son

I have written poems about my mother, father, grandfather, neighbors, lovers, and friends, but

I have written no poems about my son.

My feelings about him
are entirely uncomplicated.

Perhaps that's why

my mother has written no poems about me.

Sore Feet

—Little girls need saddle shoes
and Easter Sunday t-straps,
capped toes and leather soles,
and Mary Janes—you said
about the hand-me-down clogs in purple suede
with *Made in Denmark* stamped on the sole
that I loved more than anything.

—Your feet will spread!—you cried
as I ran barefoot outside
—They need support!—
I imagined my feet
spreading wider and wider,
becoming a fin,
The Little Mermaid played backwards.

A girl sometimes needs
a different kind of support.

Purple suede clogs or nothing.

Mother, Making Ends Meet

—They just can't seem to make ends meet—
and standing in the twilight kitchen
sighing about what's left over
she eats the meat gone grey and curling,
sated by my watching of her
glistening with sacrifice.

I'm not sure what this ends meat is,
but I've a different appetite.

Captain

My father pressed two pills
from a crackling blister pack
taking one
and breaking one
and giving half each to my sister and me,
placing the white pieces into our outstretched hands
as though we were communicants
and he a priest in Sunday-dad sneakers.
—It might make you sleepy
but you won't get sea-sick.—

And we didn't.

I do not remember seeing any whales.

I do remember returning to the Chevy Impala
in the parking lot by the harbor
my hot skin and my sister's
sticking to the naugahyde seats
as we looked to our father
to know what was next.

—Just let me sit for a minute—
and he was asleep.

Emergency Preparedness

I did not complain when told lights out,
just retreated under the covers
with a flashlight and Nancy Drew

and when the batteries died I would creep
downstairs to the kitchen drawer storing
flashlights, batteries, candles, matches
and take what I needed.

Once, towards the end of a quiet winter
there was a blizzard
and in the dark my father went
to the drawer of emergency supplies
to discover all the batteries gone, the flashlights useless.

Ex-Navy, he was troubled by this failure of preparedness
more than another man might have been

and I felt bad for having made him uneasy
but not very
because an early bedtime
with no flashlight would have been
the real emergency.

Main Street

Ruby lived on the other side of Main Street
with her older brother,
not much looked after
by their grandmother, Virginia
Slims and solitaire
at the kitchen table in a bathrobe all day long.

Ruby's brother had curly dark hair and
I wasn't sure why
I felt nervous as I watched him devour
slice after slice of Wonder Bread with Skippy, drink
milk right from the carton
silent, concentrating, like a wolf.

Ruby's family was the first I knew to get HBO and even though
we only watched *Sergeant Pepper's Lonely Heart's Club Band,*
Ruby said you could also watch movies of people having sex.
She never had but wanted to
but her parents would find out because of the bill.
She hadn't yet decided whether or not it was worth it.

My parents said—Don't go to Ruby's house. Don't cross
that busy street! You could get hit by a car.
We are very worried
you could get hit by a car.—

I went anyway and wondered
if the real reason I wasn't supposed to go
was the HBO
or the feeling I got when I looked at Ruby's brother.

Ruby got encephalitis, from a mosquito bite.
She didn't die. She didn't get better.
This made me so angry at my parents although
I never told them:

They should have known.
They should have known that
Virginia Slims and
movies of people having sex and
a boy with curly hair
and cars
were nothing to worry about.

Nothing at all.

Italian Movie Star

I watched you through the window as you
spread nets over your strawberry plants whose
glittering gems brought the birds from the sky.
I collected your mail while you
took pictures of the Colosseum and the Sistine Chapel.
When the occasional tennis ball flew over the fence
from your back-yard court,
like a Labrador I retrieved it.

By the time I was fourteen I was no longer impressed

until one day you appeared in nothing but a slip
feet bloodied from walking barefoot through the snow
weeping, mascara streaking your face, chest heaving
magnificent as an Italian movie star
like the ones I saw speaking in subtitles
on the Classics Channel.
—He's left me! He's left me for another woman!—

There was no one else to help you, and so I walked you home
to your husband who cried—Thank God!
She's been getting worse and worse and sometimes
just wanders off.—

You looked at him with nothing
in your eyes, unsure who he was.
—There, there, love—he said—Let me draw you a bath—
and he led you away
confused but compliant.

In my adolescent cruelty
I was disappointed.

Is That All There Is?

Wineglasses—empty, crusty, blushed with rust—
watch dully as I, empty, acquiesce
to our undressing as we don't caress,
to unambitious kisses, listless lust.

A careless wrestler crashing to the mat,
you take me in a tumble on the floor
and satisfy your mandate, nothing more,
as passionate as any bureaucrat.

My expectations were already low—
a sexy slumber party, maybe brunch—
but sadly even that was just too much
for you, my darling. So get dressed and go!

I hope that by tomorrow I can laugh at it—
to want so little and not to get the half of it.

Mistaken Identity

"Welcome, Mr., Mrs.! Take your key—
and with our compliments, I'm pleased to say
your room has been upgraded to a suite
for honey-mooners. Please, enjoy your stay!"

In the lobby bar, you take my hand.
We sip and smile and toast our holiday,
and when we reach our room, we find it grand
(and still we jump in bed without delay).

But any bar can serve me a martini;
the lobby store sells robes that bear the name
of the hotel. There really isn't any
reason, save for one, I want to stay:

For here in this hotel I am your Mrs.,
but after we check out . . . someone else is.

The Bathroom Door

Familiarity might tempt
a lover to show his contempt
for his beloved, so it's said,
but nearness makes my love instead
grow stronger. Socks tossed to the floor,
the left-wide-open bathroom door,
the counter's ruby wine-glass ring,
our small domestic messes bring
me joy. You've dropped all your defences,
packed away love's proud pretences.
Careless closeness shows to me
your sureness of love's constancy.
I can't hope you'll view me so kindly;
I shut the bathroom door behind me.

The Stingy Carver

When you prepare a meal for us, your art
consists of how you weigh out every part
of passion's feast, dish out in proper measure
the portions, sized to optimize our pleasure.

When I am in the kitchen, I'm unable
to show restraint, and so, upon the table
I heap the meat in trembling piles until
the only cut that's absent is my skill.

Your plate with every morsel I can gather
is filled, the platter scraped so I can slather
upon your bread the whole of me, despite
your clearly over-sated appetite.

When next I'm moved to serve to you my heart,
I'll learn the stingy carver's cunning art.

Facing-Page Translation

I am in bed, reading
a book of poems.
Or at least,
I am reading the right-hand pages
on which the poems' translations into English appear.

I can't read Arabic.

But I am drawn to the left-hand pages,
beautiful and inscrutable, and
I almost believe
they might reveal their secrets
if only I look hard and long enough.

On the other side of the bed, you read
The Economist,
silent.

Homecoming

Coming home to you after
I was unfaithful
felt like coming home
from a trip abroad:
what had once been familiar seemed foreign
until it didn't anymore and
it was just home again.

Because you have no interest in travel,
I didn't tell you
where I had been or
what I had done there.

You didn't seem to notice
that I had gone
anywhere at all.

Guest

You brought home a snake as though
there were not already enough
dangers under our roof.
It curls and uncurls in a tank
in the guest room where you sleep
as though you were a guest.

The crickets it eats you put
in the master bedroom where I sleep
as though I were the master.

They sound the alarm.

In Costa Rica

Our son says
—Of all land animals, howler monkeys
have the loudest call.
They don't often fight, but when they do
they sometimes really hurt each other.—

What else did he learn
when we put him in front of the television
to watch David Attenborough
long enough for us to have a quiet argument,
our voices straining not to be heard
above the howl?

The cleaner, brusque, pressed
an orange arrow—stain here—
clucked—might not come out—

looked into my eyes, softened.
Tears are tough, but we will try.

Sometimes, Going in Circles Is the Way Out

Although our conversation died many blocks ago
we continue our walk north on Bathurst Street
and I notice for the first time
a circle of lawn at Wolseley Street,
a hopeful green despite the late autumn date.
Tracks circumscribe it:
here a streetcar can change direction
without going backwards,
without any trouble at all.

A Vision

I see you being leaned into by her.
I see you being whispered to by her.
I see you being made to laugh,
I see you in the aftermath
of being left by me.

Animal

Dog, you are a priest—
plastic collar can't stop
you licking your itches
your stitched-up wishes
and breaking your too-short leash.

Roommates

We meet through the bland urgency of necessity
vaguely curious
mildly apprehensive
ultimately apathetic
yet compelled to make peace with our intimacy.

We are not lovers, seeking to obliterate our separateness,
sinking sighing into each other's empty spaces.
We are not friends, spontaneous in solidarity,
meeting, speaking freely, parting.
Unambitious, we wish only not to be inconvenienced,
and, in more expansive moments, not to cause inconvenience.
Our generosity with each other extends no further than this.

We circle each other, now amiable, now uneasy,
taking stock of our differences.
In the kitchen, you crunch organic granola,
reproach my Pop-Tart choice.
Your pot of chives, cheerful and forceful,
crowds my tulips on the sill to witness sequential solitary suppers,
dishes done twice.
Tupperware cupping tomorrow's lunch
teeters on the fridge's shelf
all night.

I listen for you in the bathroom; you listen for me.
We take polite turns:
the gushing of water, the brushing of teeth,
the silence of self-examination in the medicine-cabinet mirror.
We bear indifferent witness to our bodies' disintegrations:

I stretch your hair, a sodden seaweed tangle, from the drain.
You swipe epidermal scum; the tub shines behind your sponge.
You sweep nail parings from the floor.

We do not make a home.

Marrow

I don't think that when Thoreau said he wanted
to live deep and suck out all the marrow of life
he meant what I mean
when I'm sitting in Gerry's Bar in the *Grand Hotel et de Milan* and
letting the glistening center of a veal shank
slide out onto saffron risotto.

The bottle of prosecco glistens in its bucket,
shifts comfortably on the ice,
wears a white linen napkin around its neck.
We gossip about our neighbors:
of the expensively-dressed and bored Russian women
waiting for their tardy husbands you say
—Nobody know how to wait like those women.
They are only 30, but they have been waiting for centuries.—
We decide that the generously-figured Italian woman whose
clothes from Zara are made Prada-fabulous by her sprezzatura
is not sleeping with the man with whom she is engaged
in deep conversation—brother? colleague?

We slurp our prosecco, our risotto.
I lift the shank, empty now,
and suck it nonetheless.

Oh, Thoreau!
This is no life of quiet desperation:
this is marrow, too.

Freedom

While they serve their sentence
of childhood and adolescence,
our happiness is interrupted only
by the occasional but inevitable
bout of melancholy
(we are human, after all)
easily remedied by
any number of pleasures:

call in sick and spend the day in bed
with a big Russian novel
or a big Russian, as is your pleasure;
pass the afternoon in a museum
or in a bar;
spend a hundred dollars on a perfect
crimson lipstick—
any of these things will make you
feel better

and if they don't, well,
you must have had a permissive
childhood—been told to follow your bliss, allowed
to run around barefoot with uncombed hair,
to fall asleep on the floor without saying your prayers.

You must serve your sentence now and I'm sorry
to say it will be a lot longer—
adulthood stretches on for years and years and you will discover
that there are no joys other
than sex and books and drinks—at least none as reliable
as these freedoms into which the passing of childhood releases
you.

And to the children at their prayers,
I smile and whisper,
Don't worry—
one day you'll get yours.

About the Author

Mary-Michelle DeCoste grew up in Dover, Massachusetts. She received her BA in Comparative Literature from the University of Massachusetts Amherst and her PhD in Romance Studies from Cornell University. She is the author of a book on Boiardo and Ariosto (*Hopeless Love,* University of Toronto Press, 2009) and numerous articles on topics in Italian literature. Her poems have been published in journals such as *Third Wednesday, The Lyric,* and *Mezzo Cammin.* She lives in Guelph, Ontario, where she is Associate Professor of Italian Studies at the University of Guelph.

www.ingramcontent.com/pod-product-compliance
Lightning Source LLC
Chambersburg PA
CBHW071642090426
42738CB00013B/3184